A Gift

PRESENTED TO:

_____

FROM:

_____

DATE:

_____

Published by C. R. Gibson®
C. R. Gibson® is a registered trademark of Thomas Nelson, Inc., Nashville, Tennessee 37214

Designed by Anderson Thomas Design, Nashville, Tennessee.

Printed in China

GB4164
ISBN: 0-7667-6662-4

For Your
GRADUATION

Contents

Foreword

First of all, congratulations! You made it. You are now part of the real world (no, not that one – the "real" real world). Soon you'll experience all the freedom that comes from being a fully functioning, self-reliant adult. On the other hand, you're also about to discover the myriad responsibilities, challenges, and uncertainties independence and adulthood brings.

While years of formal schooling have equipped you with the tools to succeed in life, you will soon discover that the wisdom you have gained from your parents, close relatives, teachers, and others mentors will be your greatest asset when it's time to make critical, life-changing decisions.

You will also draw on the wealth of knowledge you have gained from such unique life-experiences as challenges you have overcome, books and movies you have enjoyed, and friendships you have formed.

Believe it or not, although this rich tapestry of memories, convictions, and ideas are fresh in your mind today, they can soon fade with time. Although you are busy with countless details preparing for the rest of your life, take a few minutes to fill in the pages that follow. Someday (maybe sooner than you think) you will be grateful that you made the effort to record your feelings at this very important season of your life. And who knows. The person you are today may need to remind the person you are then just what is important in life.

Remembrance of
THINGS PAST

When I was young I felt so small
And frightened for the world was tall.

And even grasses seemed to me
A forest of immensity.

Until I learned that I could grow,
A glance would leave them far below.

Spanning a tree's height with my eye,
Suddenly I soared as high,

And fixing on a star I grew,
I pushed my head against the blue!

Still, like a singing lark, I find
Rapture to leave the grass behind.

And sometimes standing in a crowd
My lips are cool against a cloud.

– Anne Morrow Lindbergh

Record a few of your earliest memories. Note how these experiences have made you the person you are today.

There is always one moment in childhood when the door opens and lets the future in.

—Graham Greene

Life is not a having and a getting, but a being and a becoming.

– Matthew Arnold

4

our family – your parents, your grandparents, your siblings, and your extended family – are integral parts of who you are today. Describe how their advice, encouragement, and humor has had an impact on your life.

We never

know the love

of the parent

until we

become

parents

ourselves.

–Henry Ward

Beecher

_____
_____
_____
_____
_____
_____
_____
_____
_____
_____
_____
_____
_____
_____
_____
_____
_____

_People travel
the world
over in search
of what they
need and then
return home
to find it._

_–George
Moore_

6

HOME IS WHERE
ONE STARTS FROM.

–T. S. ELIOT

riendships arise out of shared circumstances, shared interests, and shared memories. While some friendships burn brightly for a time and then quickly dim, others last for years – even a lifetime. List your closest friends and note the memorable events and heartfelt conversations that have forged a special bond. Imagine where your friends will be in 10 years, 20 years, or longer.

We cannot tell

the precise

moment when

friendship is

formed. As in

filling a vessel

drop by drop,

there is at last

a drop which

makes the

heart run over.

—James

Boswell

Friendship consists of forgetting what one gives, and remembering what one receives.

–Alexandre Dumas

A teacher is anyone who shares their particular knowledge on a particular subject in a way that makes it particularly interesting to you.

Teachers can be found in schools, libraries, and churches. But, in reality, they are anyone who loves to unselfishly illuminate the world to those around them. Note some of your favorite teachers and the vital lessons they have taught you.

Teachers

affect eternity,

they can

never tell

where their

influence

stops.

– from Henry

Brook Adams

_____

_____

_____

_____

_____

_____

_____

_____

_____

_____

_____

_____

_____

_____

Great teachers
never strive to
explain their
vision – they
simply invite
you to stand
beside them
and see for
yourself.

–from

R. Inman

Embracing the
PRESENT
MOMENT

We have tomorrow
Bright before us
Like a flame.

Yesterday
A night-gone thing,
A sun-down name.

And dawn-today
Broad arch above the road we came.

We march!

–Langston Hughes

our life, quite literally, is a gift. When you consider the countless events that had to occur over the centuries to bring you into the world the odds are incalculable. As you reflect on the person you are today do you believe you have made the most of this tremendous gift you have been given. Over the next few pages describe the accomplishments, attitudes, and personality traits about yourself you are most happy with and proud of. Then make a list of areas you would like to improve upon over the next few years.

The present

is the point

at which

time touches

eternity.

–C. S. Lewis

_____

_____

_____

_____

_____

_____

_____

_____

_____

_____

_____

The essence of greatness is the perception that virtue is enough.

–Ralph Waldo Emerson

Determine

the thing

that can and

shall be done,

and then we

shall find

the way.

–Abraham

Lincoln

There are no rules of architecture for a castle in the clouds.

–G.K. Chesterton

18

EVERY SITUATION – NO,
EVERY MOMENT – IS OF
INFINITE WORTH; FOR IT IS
THE REPRERESENTATIVE OF
A WHOLE ETERNITY.

–JOHANN WOLFGANG VON GOETHE

*P*ersonal tastes, like the styles upon which they are based, are often fleeting and soon forgotten. Take a moment to note your favorite movie, book, color, clothing item, song and musical group, actor and actress, and other notable pop culture icons. Someday you'll either look back and note with satisfaction what great taste you had as a young adult or ask yourself, "What was I thinking?!?"

Could we teach taste or genius by rules, they would no longer be taste or genius.

—Joshua Reynolds

Proper words in proper places make the true definition of style.

–Jonathan Swift

THOUGH WE TRAVEL THE
WORLD OVER TO FIND
THE BEAUTIFUL, WE MUST
CARRY IT WITH US OR WE
FIND IT NOT.
–RALPH WALDO EMERSON

In search of TODAY'S vision for TOMORROW

I never loved your plains,
　　Your gentle valleys,
Your drowsy country lanes
　　And pleached alleys.

I want my hills – the trail
　　That scorns the hollow –
Up, up the ragged shale
　　Where few will follow.

Up, over wooded crest,
　　And mossy boulder,
With strong thigh, heaving chest,
　　And swinging shoulder.

So let me hold my way,
　　By nothing halted,
Until at close of day,
　　I stand exalted.

High on my hills of dreams –
　　Dear hills that know me!
And then how fair will seem
　　The land below me!

How pure, at vesper-time
　　The far bells chiming!
God, give me hills to climb
　　And strength for climbing!

–Arthur Guiterman

*O*ver the next few years you will be laying a foundation for your chosen profession. If you are planning on attending college or trade school, draft a plan for how this investment in time and money can be maximized in terms of knowledge increased, contacts developed, and experience gained. If you intend to enter the workforce immediately, note ways you can stand out among your peers and increase your chances for success.

Afoot and light-hearted I take to the open road, healthy, free, the world before me. The long brown path before me leading wherever I choose.

–Walt Whitman

_____

_____

_____

_____

_____

_____

_____

_____

_____

_____

_____

_____

_____

_____

_____

_____

_____

_____

There is always room at the top.

–Daniel Webster

WELCOME, O LIFE! I GO
TO ENCOUNTER FOR THE
MILLIONTH TIME THE
REALITY OF EXPERIENCE.

−JAMES JOYCE

f you are like most people, the chances are that one of your goals is to get married and establish your own family. Picture in your mind, and then record, the qualities of your ideal spouse, the number of children you would like to have, where you hope to live, what traditions you would like to preserve that are part of your heritage, and what new customs you would like to institute.

I don't know

who my

grandfather

was. I am

much more

concerned to

know what

his grandson

will be.

—Abraham

Lincoln

_____

_____

_____

_____

_____

_____

_____

_____

_____

_____

_____

_____

_____

_____

_____

_____

Parents are patterns.

–Thomas Fuller

A happy and fulfilling life includes making the most of your body and mind. From increasing your physical activity to decreasing your stress, from reading more to watching television less, there are many ways you can maximize your time and achieve a more dynamic and fruitful life. Set a few realistic goals that will stretch you physically and mentally. As the years pass your efforts will become more obviously rewarding and enriching.

A sound mind in a sound body is a short but full description of a happy state in this world.

—John Locke

An early morning walk is a blessing for the whole day.

–Henry David Thoreau

At some point in your life you will learn that the most valuable asset you possess is the character of your heart and the quality of your moral fiber. Like anything of real worth, virtue is something that must be cherished, exercised, and refined on a daily basis. List the qualities you find most admirable in a person and how you can perfect these attributes in yourself. You might also note the characteristics of positive role models you know personally or have read about.

Free will, though it makes evil possible, is also the only thing that makes possible any love of goodness or joy worth having.

–C. S. Lewis

Always do right. This will gratify some people, and astonish the rest.

–Mark Twain

36

If you sit down at set of sun
And count the acts that you have done
    And counting, find
One self-denying deed, one word
That eased the hearts of those who heard
    One glance most kind,
That fell like sunshine where it went
Then you may count that day well spent.

–George Eliot

At this point in your life, the future lies before you as a seemingly endless highway of golden opportunities, second chances, and divergent paths. Yet time is deceptively fleeting and the time we are allotted is never certain. Picture yourself as a person of advanced age who is reflecting upon their life. What choices are you making today that will cause the person you are then to look back with gladness or regret? List ten resolutions that you feel confident will serve you throughout your life, regardless of unexpected disappointments and blessings you encounter along the way.

Life can only be understood backwards, but it must be lived forwards.

—Sören Kierkegaard

39

I resolve to live with all my might while I do live, and as I shall wish I had done ten thousand years hence.

–Jonathan Edwards

Never, never, never, never give up.

–Winston Churchill

I EXPECT TO PASS THROUGH THIS
WORLD BUT ONCE. ANY GOOD
THEREFORE THAT I CAN DO OR
ANY KINDNESS THAT I CAN SHOW
FOR ANY FELLOW CREATURE, LET ME
DO IT NOW. LET ME NOT DEFER
OR NEGLECT IT, FOR I SHALL NOT
PASS THIS WAY AGAIN.

–RALPH WALDO EMERSON

AUTOGRAPHS AND SPECIAL THOUGHTS, FROM FAMILY, FRIENDS, AND TEACHERS.

46

To everything there is as season,
A time for every purpose under heaven.

A time to be born,
  And a time to die;
A time to plant,
  And a time to pluck what is planted;
A time to kill,
  And a time to heal;
A time to break down,
  And a time to build up;
A time to weep,
  And a time to laugh;
A time to mourn,
  And a time to dance;
A time to cast away stones;
  And a time to gather stones;
A time to embrace,
  And a time to refrain from embracing;
A time to gain,
  And a time to lose;
A time to keep,
  And a time to throw away;
A time to tear,
  And a time to sew;
A time to keep silence,
  And a time to speak;
A time to love,
  And a time to hate;
A time of war,
  And a time of peace.

—Ecclesiastes 3:1-8